EXTREME 3-D

WILD WEATHER

By Jackie Ball

■SCHOLASTIC

Published by Tangerine Press, an imprint of
Scholastic Inc.,
557 Broadway, New York, NY 10012
Scholastic Canada Ltd., Markham, Ontario
Scholastic Australia Pty. Ltd, Gosford NSW
Scholastic New Zealand Ltd., Greenmount, Auckland

an imprint of
SCHOLASTIC
www.scholastic.com

Scholastic and Tangerine Press and associated
logos are trademarks of Scholastic Inc.

Produced by becker&mayer!
11120 NE 33rd Place, Suite 101
Bellevue, WA 98004
www.beckermayer.com

becker&mayer!
BOOK PRODUCERS

If you have questions or comments about this product, please visit www.beckermayer.com/customerservice and click on
Customer Service Request Form.

Edited by Ben Grossblatt
Cover designed by Shane Hartley
Book interior designed by Rosanna Villarta
Design assistance by Mathew McInelly and Bill Whitaker
Product development by Brandon Walker and Chris Tanner
Production management by Larry Weiner
Photo research by Zena Chew
All rights reserved.

Photo credits: Title page: Tornado striking town © Alan R Moller/Stone/Getty Images; **Page 5:** Students battle a fierce
headwind © AP Photo/Lawrence Journal-World/Thad Allender; cycle rickshaws © AP Photo/Pavel Rahman; **Page 8:**
Sandstorm © Andrew McConnell/Robert Harding World Imagery/Getty Images; **Page 9:** Train swept off the tracks © AP
Photo/Kerstin Joensson; **Page 10:** Hurricane Katrina, satellite image from NOAA; **Page 11:** Car crushed by a tree © Robert
Sullivan/AFP/Getty Images; **Page 12:** Hurricane waves © Angelo Cavalli/The Image Bank/Getty Images; **Page 13:** People
waiting for rescue boat © Guy Reynolds/Dallas Morning News/Corbis; boat displaced by Hurricane Katrina, by Mark Wolfe/
FEMA; **Page 14:** Index-Galena Road, by Marvin Nauman/FEM; **Page 15:** Livestock, by Andrea Booher/FEMA; flooded street,
by Jocelyn Augustino/FEMA; **Page 16:** Manitoba tornado © Wave RF/Photolibrary; **Page 17:** Store damaged by a tornado ©
Alex Wong/Getty Images News; home destroyed by a tornado © Joe Raedle/Getty Images News; **Page 18:** Tornado funnel,
Xenia, Ohio © AP Photo/Fred Stewart; **Page 19:** Waterspout © James M. Heston/AFP/Getty Images; double twister © Frank
Stahlberg; **Page 20:** Dust storm, from the George E. Marsh Album/NOAA; **Page 23:** California firefighters © AP Photo/Mike
Meadows; helicopter dropping water on a fire, by Andrea Booher/FEMA; **Page 24:** Sled dogs © Alaskastock/Photolibrary;
Page 25: Adelie penguin, by Timothy Russer, National Science Foundation; Russian icebreaker, by Patrick Rowe, National
Science Foundation; **Page 27:** Woman shoveling snow © Whit Richardson/Aurora/Getty Images; **Page 29:** Avalanche
rescue dog © Bill Stevenson/Aurora/Getty Images; **Page 30:** Street after an ice storm © AP Photo/Dick Blume, Syracuse
Newspapers; **Page 31:** Clearing ice-covered branches © AP Photo/Charles Krupa; **Page 33:** Ice buildings © Cancan Chu/Getty
Images; **Page 34:** Oregon coast waves © Bob Pool/Photographer's Choice/Getty Images; **Page 35:** Sailboat in a storm ©
John Lund/Crush/Corbis; Earth and Moon, from NASA Images; **Page 36:** Flooded lobby at the Sea Pearl Beach Hotel © AP
Photo/ CP, Deddeda Stemler; **Page 37:** Galle, Sri Lanka © AP Photo/Elizabeth Dalziel; cleaning up after the 2004 tsunami ©
Paula Bronstein/Reportage/Getty Images; **Page 40:** Sun dog © Tony Wan Kenobi; **Page 41:** Dead coral reef © Tim Laman/
National Geographic/Getty Images; leaping tree frog © Jozsef Szentpeteri/National Geographic/Getty Images; **Page 42:** New
Orleans residents after Hurricane Katrina © AP Photo/David J. Phillip; **Page 43:** Rescuing stranded dogs, by Dave Saville/
FEMA; volunteer firefighters rescuing flood victim © AP Photo/ Waco Tribune Herald, Jerry Larson; **Page 44:** Satellite image
of forest fires, from NASA/Goddard Space Flight Center Scientific Visualization Studio; **Page 45:** Smokejumper © by Stephen
Ferry/Liaison/Getty Images; rescue planes © Stocktrek Images/Getty Images; **Page 46:** NOAA satellite launch, from the
United Launch Alliance/NOAA; **Page 47:** TOPEX/Poseidon satellite, from CNES/NASA/JPL-Caltech; satellite image of dust
over east Asia, from the SeaWiFS Project, NASA/Goddard Space Flight Center, and ORBIMAGE; **Back cover:** Hurricane Rita,
satellite image from NOAA.

01/11 Dongguan, China

Printed, manufactured, and assembled in China

10 9 8 7 6 5 4 3 2
ISBN: 978-0-545-22070-5
10392

Conforms to ASTM standard F963-08, and CPSIA.

Violent thunderstorms, hurricanes, tornadoes, blizzards, floods, and other forms of wild weather cause billions of dollars in damages and thousands of deaths and injuries throughout the world every year. We can't control the weather, and we sure can't change it. But we can learn more about it, and be prepared. And now, you can see some of the wildest weather on the planet come to life in 3-D!

Contents

WILD WEATHER 101

What makes wild weather? Blame it on the pressure Earth is under. A thick blanket of air called the *atmosphere* keeps pressing down on us, sometimes hard and sometimes lightly. When the atmospheric pressure changes, so does the weather.

This cloud's real name is cumulonimbus, but there's another word for it: *trouble*. Clouds like this mean storms are on the way.

Wild Weather Ingredient #1: Wind

Wind is moving air. It's created when air warmed by the Sun rises and the space it occupied is replaced by cooler air. When a large mass of cold air collides with a large mass of warm air, the most extreme weather conditions can occur. The line where these masses meet is called a *front*.

50 mph (80 kph) winds prop up middle schoolers in Lawrence, Kansas.

Wild Weather Ingredient #2: Water

Water is continually recycled. Water in oceans, lakes, and puddles is heated by the Sun and changes to a gas called water vapor through a process called *evaporation*. The vapor rises into the atmosphere, cools, and turns back into liquid droplets. The droplets bunch together to form clouds. When clouds become too heavy, they break apart and fall to the ground as rain, snow, or sleet—then evaporation begins again.

Cycle rickshaws make their way through flooded streets in Dhaka, Bangladesh.

THAT'S WILD! There is exactly the same amount of water on Earth as there ever was—no more, no less.

LIGHTNING

Lightning is a tremendous spark of static electricity that leaps from cloud to cloud, from one part of the sky to another, or from a cloud to the ground. It's produced when water droplets and tiny pieces of ice inside a cloud rub against one another. This rubbing, called *friction*, creates an electrical charge.

A bolt of lightning is five times hotter than the surface of the sun!

Ancient Greeks believed that lightning bolts were hurled down from Mt. Olympus by their chief god, Zeus.

Loud Weather
Thunder is the sound of air molecules exploding away from each other as lightning is formed. We see lightning before we hear thunder because light travels faster than sound.

THAT'S WILD!
To figure out how far away a thunderstorm is, count the seconds from a lightning flash to the crash of thunder, then divide that number by five. That's about how many miles away the lightning struck. (To find out about how many kilometers away the lightning struck, divide by three instead.) For example, if you hear the thunder 8 seconds after you see the lightning, the storm is about 1.6 miles away ($8 \div 5 = 1.6$).

EXTREME WINDS

On highways, strong winds can push tractor trailers across four lanes and slam them down onto their sides. In cities, they can send pieces of glass and metal flying like bullets. In the country, powerful winds snap trees and power lines, blocking roads, smashing roofs, and leaving residents without heat or light for days. And in desert areas such as this one near the Sudanese border in Eritrea, Africa, high winds can cause sandstorms, amazingly high walls of sand that move at speeds of up to 70 mph (113 kph), scouring every exposed surface and erasing entire cities from view.

Sandstorms are common in areas where the temperature is high and rainfall is scarce.

Windy City

In a city, high winds can cause minor problems, like broken umbrellas, or life-or-death emergencies. In 2008, nine people in New York City perished in two separate wind-related accidents that involved cranes crashing to the ground from high-rise construction sites.

A heavy storm in Austria swept this train right off the rails!

You're Cleared for Takeoff

Extremely high winds can be dangerous, but they can also give a real lift to an extreme sport like windsurfing. However, this windsurfer had better watch the clouds. Their tops are white, but their undersides are dark—meaning the water molecules inside are packed together too tightly to let light through. It's only a matter of time before they break apart as rain.

THAT'S WILD!

The highest winds ever measured at Earth's surface—not including winds inside tornadoes—occurred on Australia's Barrow Island. In 1996, Tropical Cyclone Olivia unleashed winds of 253 mph (407 kph) on the tiny island.

HURRICANES

A hurricane is a huge cluster of fierce thunderstorms that circle in a spiral pattern. Winds topping 74 mph (119 kph) blow constantly around the center, or eye, of the hurricane.

Not just any storm can be called a hurricane. It's a special storm that requires special ingredients. First, it must form over the ocean, and the ocean's temperature must be 80°F (27°C) or higher. The air has to be warm and moist. The storm must contain significant differences in air pressure. Last, the Coriolis effect, a weather phenomenon that makes winds spin, must be at work, too.

According to at least one study, the number of hurricanes per year has more than doubled in the past century.

In this satellite photo, all is calm and sunny inside the eye of the hurricane, clearly visible in the center of the mass of clouds.

Lean on Me

Most hurricanes start over the mild waters of the southern Atlantic Ocean, the Caribbean Sea, or the Gulf of Mexico. These bent-over palm trees show the effects of a hurricane's battering winds.

Turning Trees Into Weapons

When the ground is soaked from previous storms, a hurricane's ferocious winds can uproot trees and send them crashing into anything in their way. This car was crushed by one of hundreds of trees uprooted by Hurricane Frances in September 2004, in Boca Raton, Florida.

Two million people lost power because of electrical lines brought down by Hurricane Frances. Luckily, no one died.

STORM SURGE

Many hurricanes never make landfall. They spin out to sea, where they eventually die. But those that do hit land make a dramatic entrance, with crashing waves. The destruction doesn't end when the waves retreat. The sea can surge up to 19 ft. (6 m), causing dangerous flooding and beach erosion. Many hurricanes start as tropical storms and are "upgraded" to hurricane status if their winds reach 74 mph (119 kph).

This wave slammed into the island of Curacao in the Caribbean Sea.

Expensive and Deadly

In September 2005, Hurricane Katrina struck the Gulf Coast of the United States. This hurricane became the third-deadliest hurricane and the costliest natural disaster in U.S. history! Katrina was responsible for 1,833 deaths and $81 billion in damages. Almost half a million people were evacuated from New Orleans, Louisiana.

Although recovery has been difficult in New Orleans, many people have returned. In 2007, New Orleans had the fastest-growing population in the country.

THAT'S WILD!
The deadliest hurricane in U.S. history occurred in Galveston, Texas, in 1900. More than 6,000 people perished, and many more were injured from the effects of hurricane winds and a tidal wave in the Gulf of Mexico.

Tipping the Scales

Scientists use the Saffir-Simpson scale to classify hurricanes into five categories. Category 1 hurricanes are the weakest, with winds of 74–95 mph (119–153 kph). Category 5 hurricanes are the strongest, with winds of at least 156 mph (251 kph). Hurricane Katrina's peak winds of almost 175 mph (281.6 kph) placed it squarely in Category 5. The force of its winds and floods dragged boats from their moorings and dumped them miles away.

THE POWER OF WATER

A flood is one of the most powerful forces on the planet, able to sweep away people, buildings, and vehicles.

Floods can accompany hurricanes, but most frequently they're caused by rivers whose levels rise due to long periods of rain. In the spring, floods from rapidly melting snow in the mountains are common. When the water rises high enough to overflow its natural or human-made boundaries, you can end up with a disaster.

Floodwaters can even eat their way through slabs of paved road!

Beware of Flash Floods
A flash flood can happen in a split second, sending torrents of muddy water down a canyon or dry streambed.

Help Is at Hand

Thousands of people in the St. Louis, Missouri, area were evacuated from flooded areas in July 1993, but in this agricultural area, cows and other livestock had to be rescued, too. A total of 534 counties in 9 states were declared federal disaster areas, and more than 168,000 people were affected.

Underwater Street

During a flood, streets in towns and cities become waterways, navigable only by boat.

This street in Fenton, Missouri, is well named!

THAT'S WILD!

A massive flood in Johnstown, Pennsylvania, on May 31, 1889, remains one of the worst disasters in U.S. history. A dam upstream of the town failed after days of heavy rainfall, spilling 20 million tons (more than 18 million metric tons) of water. More than 2,200 people lost their lives.

TORNADOES

Like a hurricane, a tornado is a powerful storm with swirling winds. However, there is no calm eye at the center of a tornado. It's a cone of furious wind spinning from 40 mph (64 kph) to more than 300 mph (482.8 kph). A weak tornado can break branches off trees. A strong one can blow cars into the air and roofs off houses. The hail and lightning that often accompany tornadoes cause as much damage as the winds. About 1,500 tornadoes hit the United States every year.

Tornadoes begin in severe thunderstorms. Winds high in the cloud blow faster than winds that are lower in the cloud. Sometimes the winds blow in different directions, making the air spin and building up power at the cloud's center. The bottom of the cloud stretches into a point and touches the ground.

THAT'S WILD!

A group of tornadoes is called an *outbreak*. The deadliest tornadoes in U.S. history occurred during the outbreak of 1925, in which 689 people in Missouri, Illinois, and Indiana lost their lives. *The winds were so strong they blew the feathers off chickens!*

What's Left Behind

Tornadoes can be selective in what they snatch up and what they leave behind. In 1917, a tornado was reported to have carried a jar of pickles 25 mi. (40 km)—then dropped the jar without breaking it.

A resident helps clean up debris after three tornadoes ripped through central and southeastern Virginia on April 29, 2008. The roof and most of the building's interior have been blown away, but the front wall is still standing.

In Lady Lake, Florida, a couple looks over their destroyed home after thunderstorms brought powerful tornadoes through the area on February 3, 2007. At least 19 people lost their lives.

Finally—Some Good News!

Although the number of tornadoes seems to be increasing, the number of people who lose their lives in tornadoes is going down. That may be a result of better early warning systems and increased scientific knowledge about these storms.

THE 1974 SUPER OUTBREAK

On April 3, 1974, a group of 148 tornadoes swept through 13 states and parts of Canada in the 1974 Super Outbreak. In only 16 hours, the murderous storm corkscrewed across almost 2,500 mi. (4,023 km) of land. The tornado that struck Xenia, Ohio, was full of swirling black pieces. People thought swarms of blackbirds had been sucked into the funnel, but the black pieces were shingles ripped from countless roofs. Tornadoes take their color from the dirt and waste they carry.

A tornado funnel roaring through Xenia, Ohio, in 1974.

WATERSPOUTS

A waterspout is a tornado that occurs over a lake or ocean. It begins the same way as a regular tornado: a center of low air pressure causes winds to whirl, forming a rotating cloud. However, instead of ending in a funnel, the bottom of the cloud is a rotating column of air. When the bottom touches down, it sucks up surface water.

This waterspout touched down along the Mekong River during an afternoon storm in Phnom Penh, Cambodia.

One of the Family

Most waterspouts are between 20 and 200 ft. (5 and 50 m) around. In the northern hemisphere, most waterspouts whirl counterclockwise. In the southern hemisphere, the movement is clockwise. Waterspouts often occur in a group, called a *family*.

DROUGHT

A drought is a long period of time with no rain. In certain parts of the world, such as the western and southwestern United States, droughts are part of the typical weather pattern. Some cities in Arizona and California receive only a few inches of rain a year. Desert plants can survive long dry periods, but crops need constant watering to grow. Without rain to cool things down, heat builds up—and so does the risk of wildfires.

Sometimes, weather can be predictable. In parts of Asia and Africa, there is a predictable rainy and dry season every year. However, droughts can be unpredictable. In the midwestern United States, a drought lasting from 1931 to 1938 ruined crops and caused widespread devastation, poverty, and homelessness. This was known as the Dust Bowl.

In the Dust Bowl drought of the 1930s, dried topsoil blew in enormous clouds over the flat land, piling up in people's living rooms. Some storms were so powerful they carried dirt all the way to the East Coast, more than a thousand miles away.

Baked Dry

Drought bakes the earth, killing plants and drying up water supplies for people and animals. If a drenching storm breaks the dry spell, dried-up waterways like these can fill up, overflow, and become dangerous flash floods.

Looking for Water

When the dry season starts in June, African elephants migrate to places near rivers and watering holes. They return to their winter territory in November, when the rainy season begins and plants grow back. This yearly migration gives grazing areas time to regenerate.

THAT'S WILD!

When African elephants migrate at the beginning of the annual drought, they sometimes travel in huge herds containing as many as 500 members.

WILDFIRE!

In a drought, one smoldering ember from a campfire can turn a forest into an inferno. Wildfires start with dried-out brush and grasses, which ignite quickly. The fire becomes more intense, jumping to tree stumps and downed limbs and maybe even reaching up to lick at green leaves and needles. That's a disaster because evergreens such as pines and spruces have oils that burst into flames with enough heat.

If there is no rain to contain it, a brush fire, like this 2007 fire in **Southern California**, can grow and burn through millions of acres, destroying property and wildlife habitats.

THAT'S WILD!
In the southwestern region of the United States, as many as 70 percent of all forest fires begin with lightning strikes!

Fighting Fire on the Ground ...

Firefighters on the ground attack flames by beating them down, spraying them with water from portable pumps, and digging ditches to contain the blaze behind a fire line. Modern tools such as Doppler radar help scientists and firefighters track forest fires, which can save lives. However, a fire that continues for days can destroy thousands of homes and property.

Flames leap into the sky in a wall of fire near Ventura, California, in a 2005 wildfire.

... and in the Air

Airplanes have been used to fight wildfires since the California wildfires of 1919. Today, helicopters are also put to use dumping water, making observations, and sometimes transporting people in danger. However, if a gusty wind accompanies the fire, all aircraft are grounded.

A helicopter drops water on a blaze in San Diego, California.

INTENSE COLD

Antarctica is the coldest continent in the world. The temperature can sink to -128.6° F (-89.2°C). In Antarctica or anyplace, blowing wind makes it feel colder. (The effect that wind has on how cold we feel is called *wind chill*.) Heat escapes from our bodies, making the air feel colder and increasing the risks for humans. At -13° F (-25°C), with calm air, exposed skin freezes in 30 minutes. At the same temperature with a wind of 25 mph (40 kph), that time drops to 10 minutes.

Sled dogs are well-suited to life in the cold. Even so, these dogs are wearing special boots to protect their paws from the ice and cold.

That's One Way to Stop an Epidemic!

An intense cold wave struck the eastern half of the United States in February 1899. The intense cold burst water, gas, and sewer pipes sunk far underground. Chickens, sheep, and cattle froze where they stood. But one good thing happened: mosquitoes carrying the dreaded yellow fever virus froze solid, stopping an epidemic.

How do penguins survive the frigid conditions in Antarctica? A layer of fat under their skin and feathers on top provide insulation. They limit their direct contact with ice and snow by rocking back on their heels, holding their toes away from the frozen ground.

Icebreakers are needed for transporting supplies through the ice-choked waters around Antarctica.

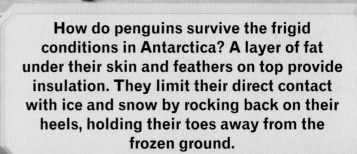

SNOW

Any snowstorm is hazardous, but a blizzard is a monster. Strong winds blow snow so hard that sometimes the whole world seems to disappear in a whiteout. This type of ferocious snowstorm often forms in late winter or early spring, when very cold, dry air collides with warm, moist air.

When snow falls, it's time for fun. It's also time to be careful. Snow leads to hundreds of deaths in the United States each year, mostly from traffic accidents, overexertion, and exposure.

The Storm of the Century

In March 1993, a blizzard called the Storm of the Century brought tornadoes, thunderstorms, and floods along with snow and wind to states from Alabama to Massachusetts.

Pile-up

One in. (2.5 cm) of rain equals 10 in. (25 cm) of snow, on average. That pile is a pain to shovel, but heaps of snow can be a help in other ways. Snow cover protects plants from harsh winter winds. Lost skiers or backpackers can survive longer in the wilderness by digging a snow cave.

Snowflakes

A snowflake starts as an ice crystal formed around a speck of dust or bacteria. All snowflakes have six sides. The fanciest ones are *dendrites*, like the snowflake shown here. Dendrites form in low clouds, where lots of moisture enables them to grow large.

THAT'S WILD!

The largest snowflake ever measured fell in Montana on January 28, 1887. It measured 15 in. (38 cm) across and was 8 in. (20 cm) thick. The most snow to fall in a one-year period in the United States was 102 ft. (31 m) at Mt. Rainier in Washington State, in 1972.

AVALANCHES

An avalanche is a raging sea of snow that slides down a mountain slope. Heavy snowfall and strong winds set the stage for an avalanche. Then all it takes is a trigger—some stress to start things rolling. Natural triggers include a falling shelf of snow. Human-created triggers can be the vibrations from snowmobiles or explosions. Sometimes avalanches are deliberately set off by explosives to control when they happen.

How fast the snow slides during an avalanche depends on the type of snow. Dry, powdery avalanches are the fastest, capable of moving more than 100 mph (160 kph). Wetter snow moves more slowly, but all avalanches can be deadly.

Avalanche Myth: Busted!
Some people think you can start an avalanche by yelling or yodeling, but that's not true. Only a noise as loud as a sonic boom can start the snow sliding.

The Nose Knows

Avalanche rescue dogs can travel over snowy areas eight times faster than humans. Speed is crucial, because chances of survival in an avalanche are only 50 percent after thirty minutes. Dogs can sniff out humans buried in snow because their more than 200 million scent cells give them a phenomenal sense of smell. They use *air-scenting* to smell human odors that rise up through the snow.

About 150 people lose their lives every year in North America and Europe. Skiers and backpackers aren't the only ones who need to worry about avalanches. Vehicles driving on mountain roads can be suddenly submerged in sliding snow, too.

ICE STORMS

Ice isn't nice. When freezing rain falls, people do, too, slipping and sliding on icy sidewalks and streets. Cars spin, planes crash, power lines snap—what makes this mess?

Under certain conditions, rain is supercooled as it falls. It freezes onto every cold surface it touches, causing inconvenience, danger, and destruction. Ice buildup on an airplane's wings or tail has caused fatal crashes. Weighted down with ice, tree limbs crack off and smash to the ground. Sometimes they take power lines with them, turning off lights and heat in neighborhoods and entire cities.

Ice-coated power lines droop under the weight in the aftermath of an ice storm in Watertown, New York.

Killer Coating
Trees weighed down by a coating of ice can fall and block roads, creating hazards for drivers.

A worker clears ice-covered branches from the road in **East Derry, New Hampshire.**

Bicycle or Icicle?
Travel of every kind comes to a halt when an ice storm strikes. Cold rain freezes when it touches cold surfaces, molding itself to the shape of whatever it hits.

THAT'S WILD!
An ice storm in January 2009 left 2 million people in the region from Oklahoma to Indiana in the dark, some of them for weeks. Worse, 55 people perished.

31

ICICLES

When dripping or flowing water freezes and refreezes, rows of icy spikes form. Icicles can look like sparkling decorations or mammoth walls of ice.

Ice Climbing

Ice climbing is a sport that depends on wild weather. Climbers use special tools to scale towering ice-coated mountains. They hammer in metal pegs called petons to pull themselves up inch by inch. They carve "steps" in the ice with axes. Claw-toothed crampons over their boots help their feet get a grip.

These frozen waterfalls are just waiting to be climbed.

Look Sharp
Glittering icicles may look stunning, but they can spell *danger*. High-hanging icicles can hurt someone if they break off and drop.

The presence of icicles can mean a house is badly insulated and leaking heat.

Icicle Festival
At the 23rd Annual Ice and Snow Festival in Harbin, Heilongjian Province, China, artists create frozen art.

THAT'S WILD!
The largest icicle ever was 36 ft. 4½ in. (11.1 m) long shand weighed 26 tons. However, it was made by humans, not nature.

MAKING WAVES

Waves are a form of endless weather created when wind blows over water. First, water rises. Then, gravity drags it down, where water pressure pushes it up again. This tug of war between water pressure and gravity continues until the wave reaches shallower water near land. Then the wave slows down, piles up, and breaks onshore. If the ocean gets shallower gradually, the wave breaks gently. If the water level drops all at once—SLAM!

Most waves come from wind blowing on the ocean. The stronger the wind and the farther it blows the water, the higher the waves.

Rogue Waves

Most waves break over land. However, waves 100 ft. (80 m) tall—as tall as the famous Rockefeller Center Christmas tree in New York City—frequently come out of nowhere on the open ocean. Scientists are studying these freak waves, which have caused deaths and injuries on cruise ships and commercial vessels.

Tide Us Over

The gravitational pull of the Sun and Moon, combined with the Earth's spin, creates tides. During a new moon or a full moon, the Sun and Moon are in a straight line, and high tides are higher.

TSUNAMI

A tsunami is a different kind of wave. Often spawned by earthquakes, these monster waves speed silently across the ocean, making not much more than a ripple on the surface. When a tsunami nears land, it slows, piles up into an enormous wall of water, and then pounds the shore.

In December 2004, about 225,000 people in Asia and Africa lost their lives from the effects of a massive tsunami triggered by an earthquake in the Indian Ocean. Scientists say the earthquake had the energy of 23,000 atom bombs.

The 2004 tsunami flooded the lobby of the Sea Pearl Beach Hotel on Phuket Island in Thailand.

The 2004 tsunami was one of the deadliest natural disasters ever. Many people lost their lives.

The tsunami left behind piles of debris in the streets of Galle, Sri Lanka.

Entire fishing villages were wiped out when the killer wave struck the beach. The tsunami destroyed about $9 billion worth of property, but the cost in human suffering is beyond calculation.

THAT'S WILD!
The highest recorded tsunami was triggered by a landslide in Lituya Bay, Alaska, on July 9, 1958. The wave reached approximately 1,700 ft. (518 m)—higher than the Washington Monument in Washington, D.C.!

SPOOKY AND STRANGE WEATHER

Hurricanes, tornadoes, and other wild weather can cause devastation. But sometimes weather is just plain weird. It can create striking scenes and surprising effects.

Fog

Fog is a cloud, so it's created when water evaporates from lakes and oceans, then cools and turns into water droplets. However, unlike other clouds, fog touches the Earth.

This photo shows sea fog over the Golden Gate Bridge in San Francisco, California. The cold Pacific Ocean is hidden from view. Sea fog can occur when warm, moist air travels over a colder surface.

It's Curtains

Auroras are curtains of glowing light above the North and South Poles. Auroras happen when electrically charged particles moving at tremendously high speeds are caught in the Earth's magnetic field. They collide with gases in the atmosphere, causing the gases to give off green, red, or purple light.

Hail, Hail

Even the biggest hailstone starts out as one tiny water droplet. The droplet rises on an updraft to the cold top of a thundercloud, where it freezes. Then it's pulled back down by warm air, thawing it. Each time the droplet bounces up and down, it adds another layer of ice.

THAT'S WILD!

The largest hailstone on record was 7 in. (18 cm) across. It fell on June 23, 2003, in Aurora, Nebraska. Hailstones can reach speeds of more than 100 mph (160 kph), smashing crops flat and making holes in roofs.

MORE SPOOKY AND STRANGE WEATHER

Sundog

Sundogs are very bright spots that sometimes appear on either side of the Sun. Sundogs are remarkable to see, but they only show up under certain circumstances. First, the Sun must be at or near the horizon. Second, it needs to be shining through a thin cloud layer. Third, six-sided ice crystals in the clouds must be lined up in a special way so the light is bent at a slight angle before we see it.

El Niño

Destructive Pattern

Every three to eight years, weather around the world is affected by a phenomenon known as *El Niño*. This condition goes along with tropical cyclones, shifts in patterns of rainfall, and a change in the eastern-blowing winds near the equator, called the *trade winds*. El Niño commonly causes droughts and floods. Scientists are still studying El Niño to better understand it.

Termperature changes during El Niño in 1998 caused this coral reef off the island of Palau in the Pacific Ocean to die.

Raining Frogs

It's Raining Cats and—Frogs?

Witnesses around the world say they've seen frogs falling from the sky. How can it be raining frogs? Scientists believe that sometimes a waterspout or a tornado sucks up frogs and fish from lakes or ponds, and then dumps them miles away.

HELP!

An extreme weather event isn't over when the fire ends or the wind stops blowing. In fact, there can be months or years of repairing, restoring, and rebuilding after the wild weather has moved on. But the first priority is rescue. Every hurricane, blizzard, tornado, flood, or other weather emergency leaves victims stranded in dangerous situations.

The people in the photo have retreated to the upper part of their house after rising waters from Hurricane Katrina flooded the bottom. They've written *SOS* on the roof to help helicopter search-and-rescue teams spot them. (Do you see the top of the red car underwater?)

Swept Away

People aren't the only victims of floods and other weather disasters. When the Tar River flooded in 1999, dozens of stranded dogs were rescued in Princeville, North Carolina.

Just in Time

Extreme weather events strike suddenly and hard. Some rescues come not a moment too soon. First responders often put their own safety at risk to save others.

EYE IN THE SKY

Imagine you're in a sailboat on the open ocean and a squall comes up, throwing you overboard. Or you're trapped on a wilderness trail in a storm, where you've been injured by falling branches. How can rescuers possibly find you?

Thanks to a search-and-rescue satellite network run by the National Oceanic and Atmospheric Administration (NOAA), help is at hand no matter where disaster strikes. Satellites over land and sea are on constant alert for distress signals from emergency beacons or personal handheld locators. When a signal is received, the emergency's location is sent to rescue teams.

Satellites can help rescuers by pinpointing the location of fires and other weather emergencies.

A satellite captured this photo of fires in 2002 at the California-Oregon border. Smoke from the fires trailed down the Pacific coast.

THAT'S WILD!
These eyes in the skies are lifesavers. As of July 2009, NOAA's satellite system has rescued more than 6,000 people in the United States. As part of a wider network with other countries, the system has helped rescue more than 24,500 people.

Smokejumpers are highly skilled firefighters who parachute into forest fire hotspots when rough terrain prevents firefighters from getting there by truck or plane. This smokejumper was participating in a 1993 practice run in Missoula, Montana.

Alaska is the state with the most rescues performed with the help of NOAA's search-and-rescue satellite system. These A-10 Thunderbolt II planes fly over the Pacific Alaska Range Complex during rescue training.

WEATHER SATELLITES

A satellite is a device that orbits the Earth and takes measurements and makes observations. Weather satellites are satellites designed to monitor cloud cover, pollution, tropical storms, and other weather phenomena. Satellites can be geostationary (they travel around the Earth at the same speed as the planet's rotation, so they are always above the same spot) or polar orbiting (they circle the planet in a loop from the North Pole to the South Pole).

The **NOAA-19** satellite was launched on February 6, 2009. The polar-orbiting satellite is designed to forecast weather, monitor forest fires and volcanic eruptions, and even track wildlife migrations!

Ocean Watcher

The TOPEX/Poseidon satellite, launched in 1992 by NASA and the French space agency CNES, took highly accurate measurements of the surface of the ocean. This information was useful for hurricane and El Niño forecasting.

TOPEX/Poseidon orbited 826 mi. (1,330 km above the Earth. The satellite stopped providing data in 2005.

Dust in the Wind

Weather satellites can monitor large-scale weather phenomena, such as this gigantic plume of dust blowing over Japan on April 2, 2002. In this image, the dust cloud is a light brown band that extends from the Asian mainland (near the upper-left corner), across the Sea of Japan, and over the Pacific Ocean.

WEATHER RECORDS

Hottest:	**136°F (58°C)**, El Azizia, Libya, on Sept. 13, 1922.
Coldest:	**-128°F (−89.2°C)**, Vostok Station, Antarctica, on July 21, 1983.
Fastest temperature drop:	**47°F (26°C) in 15 minutes**, Rapid City, South Dakota, on January 10, 1911.
Most rainfall in one minute:	**1.5 in. (38 mm)**, Barst, Guadeloupe, on November 26, 1970.
Most rainfall in one year:	**80.4 ft. (25.4 m)**, Cherrupunji, India.
Least rainfall in one year:	**0 in. (0 cm)**, Antofagasta region of Chile's Atacama Desert. Rain has never been recorded there!
Fastest wind:	**approximately 300 mph (482 kph)**, Oklahoma City, Oklahoma, on May 3, 1999. This speed was recorded by a radar unit inside a tornado!
Fastest tornado:	**73 mph (117 kph)**, during the Tri-State Tornado of 1925, a family of tornadoes that struck in Missouri, Illinois, and Indiana. This speed is the forward movement of the tornado, not the speed at which the wind spins.
Most snow in one year:	**102 ft. (31 m)**, Mt. Rainier, Washington, February 1971 to February 1972.
Biggest snowflake:	**15 in. (38 cm) across**, Fort Keough, Montana, on January 28, 1887.
Heaviest hailstone:	**2.25 lbs. (1.0 kg)**, Gopalganj District, Bangladesh, on April 14, 1986.
Biggest hailstone:	**7 in. (18 cm) across**, Aurora, Nebraska, on June 23, 2003.